A Netting Journey

Pascall Bighetty

Figure 1 The CED class of 2017

From left: Ernie (Jentzen) Sinclair, Roxanne Linklater, Sylvia Caribou, Sharona Sinclair, Dhedra Dumas, Pascall Bighetty and Terry Bear.

Back: Tommy Sinclair and Ralph Caribou.

Front: Toby Bear, Shelly Bear.

Missing: Todd Sinclair, Raven Nicholas, Tyrone.

ISBN-13: 978-0-9959291-0-4

DEDICATION

I would like to dedicate this book to the children of the earth.

Leaving the building to start the day.

CONTENTS

ACKNOWLEDGMENTS

I would like to thank Ralph Caribou, first and foremost, for giving us his time and knowledge to go out and seek some fish, "Reynold's Style!" I would also like to thank Janice Seto for making this book happen and her uplifting praise to succeed. The CED students for doing an outstanding job in the world of Netting.

1 GETTING READY

On February 12, 2017 we had planned a couple days in learning the ways of **NETTING**. The **CED** cohorts of **UCN** and our Instructor and Mentor Ralph Caribou will be guiding you through the ways of netting. **LET'S GO!**

It is important that you've had a good rest before heading out and eat a good breakfast and dress appropriately for the weather. Grab you all your gear and you're ready to step out and delve into netting glory. **LET'S GO!**

Things you will need: Your net (nets will vary depending on how much fish you want to gather), we used 100 yard net, rope, chisels, shovels, buckets, axe, knife, hookknife (to remove the fish from the net), poles and the

passion to fish. LET'S GO!

Figure 2. Leaving UCN to Get Fish

Getting to your destination varies from taking a dog team, snowshoeing or a truck. Making sure you're ready and have the necessary means to do the job safely.

Everyone is properly clothed and prepared to go. Except for the lady in the pink rubbers.

02/12/2017 21:28

On our way to our designated spot

Found a place to start chiseling our 1st hole.

Found our spot to set our net and have begun to chisel 1 of two holes. We had a good team of volunteer to chisel, clear the snow and search for 2 poles.

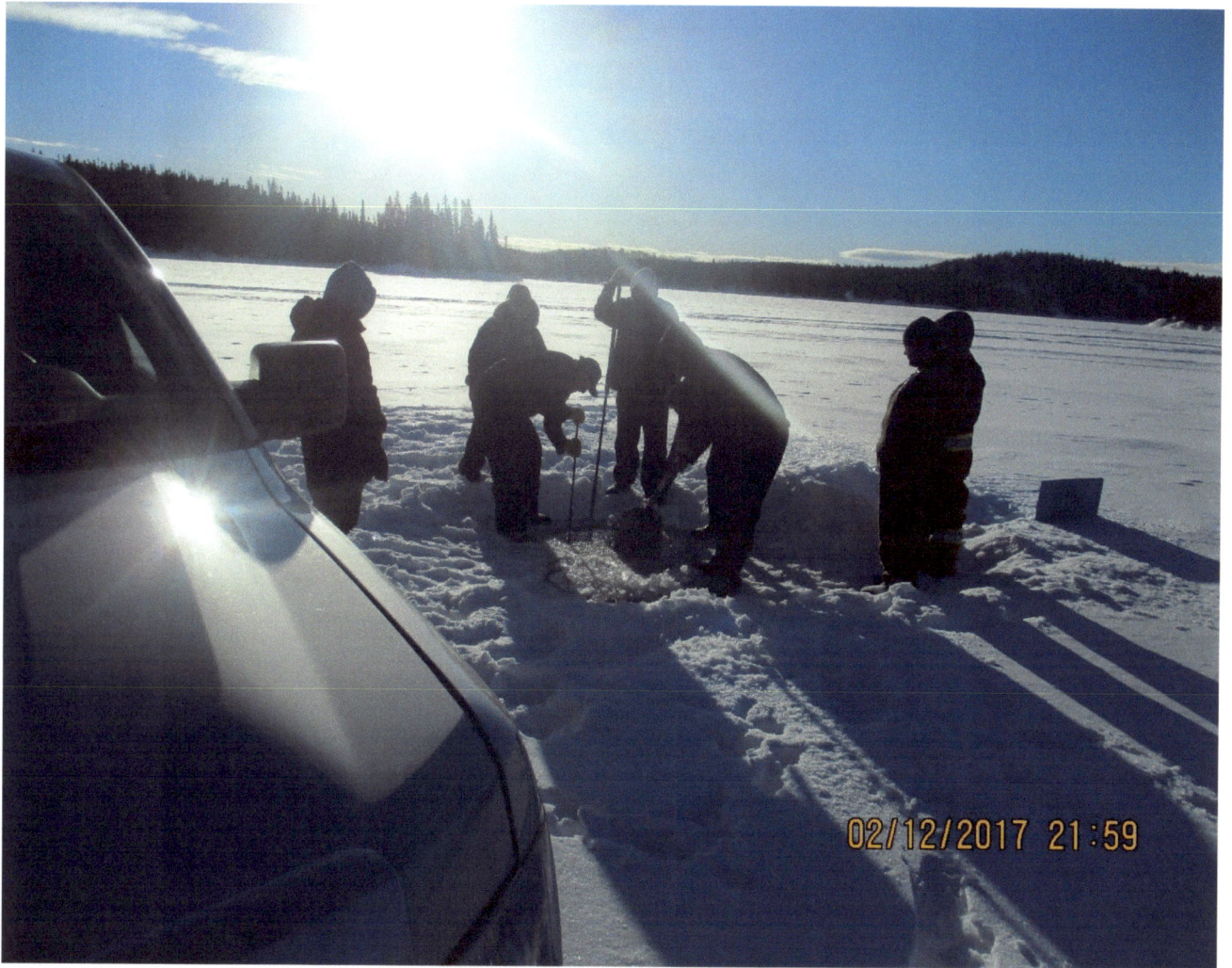

Making our 1st hole and clearing.

02/12/2017 22:27

w/Roxanne, dressed so warm she can take 5 on the snow.

Figure 3 Preparing one of two ice holes. Hole #2.w/ Sylvia, Tommy , Terry, Ralph and Ernie.

Figure 4 Locating the jig to that's attached to our line. Hole #2. w/ Shelly, Terry, Ralph and Sylvia.

Make sure you have someone follow the jig until it stops and there you chisel the 2nd hole to retrieve the jig and net line. As soon as you get the jig out, remove it from the net line and proceed to the next job, setting your net.

Pulling the line while the others are setting net.

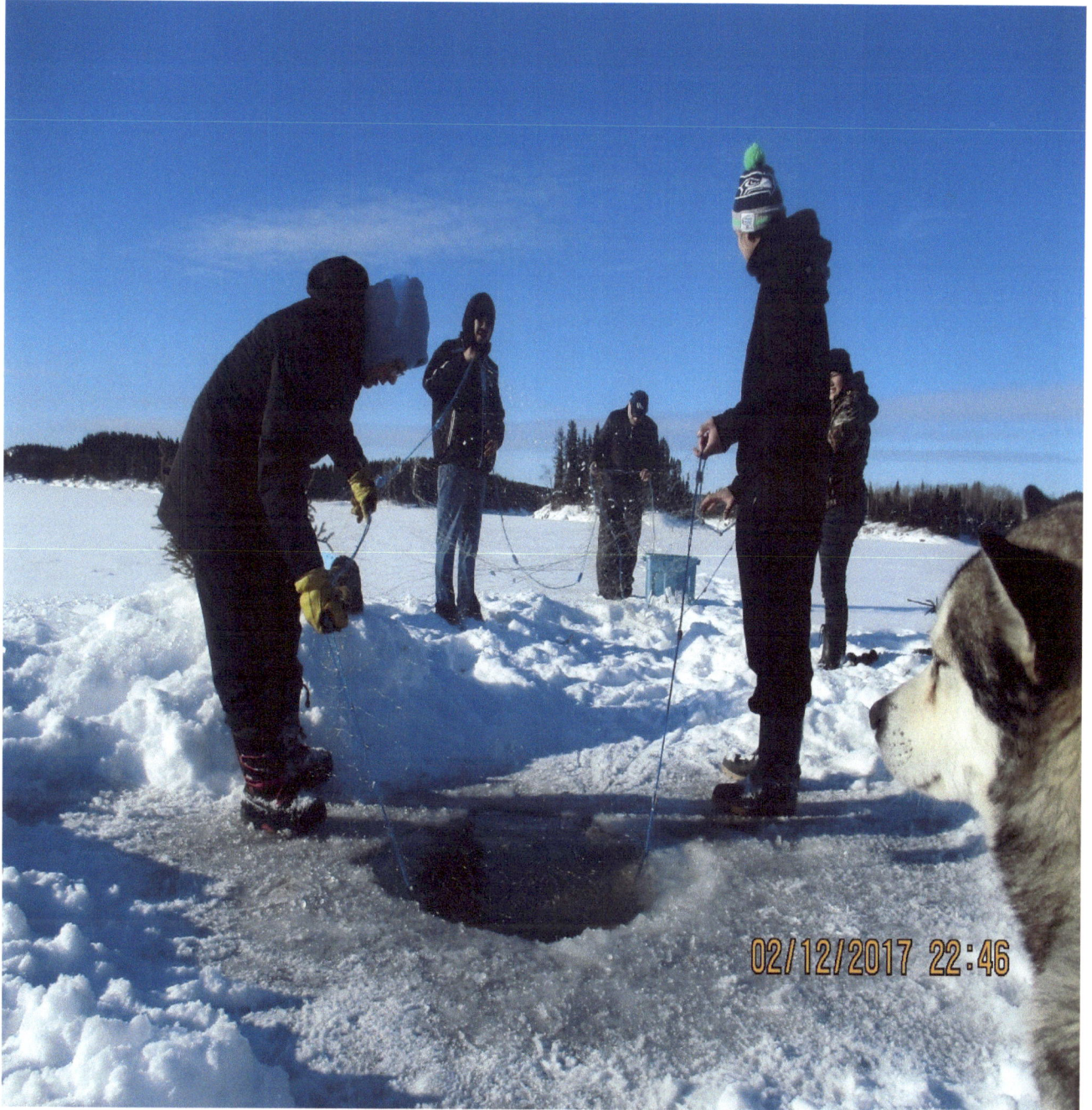

Setting the net from hole 1 while the other is pulling the line and net from the other side.

w/Tyrone Caribou, just finished pulling the net and removing line from pole.

02/13/2017 22:22

Day 2, off to retrieve our net after an overnight setting.

Here is some of our catch.

Figure 6: Getting a bird's eye view (Warrior style) of the crew while Toby and I were getting the poles. Along with our steel horse and pet.

w/ Toby Bear and our poles.

.

After all is said and done we all agreed to share our catch with the elders of Pukatawagan, Manitoba. A tradition passed from generation to generation.

Figure 8: Here we have Adelaide Bighetty (medicine woman) happily holding a walleye, w/ Sharona, Roxanne, Tyronne, Sylvia and Toby offering a little extra.

Figure 9 "Butch" filling in for his grandpa. w/Tyronne and Sylvia, Danny Daniels.

Mrs. Lena Colomb

02/13/2017 23:39

Victoria (Mrs. Moon) Bear.

Right: Mary Ann Dumas. Left: Dhedra Dumas

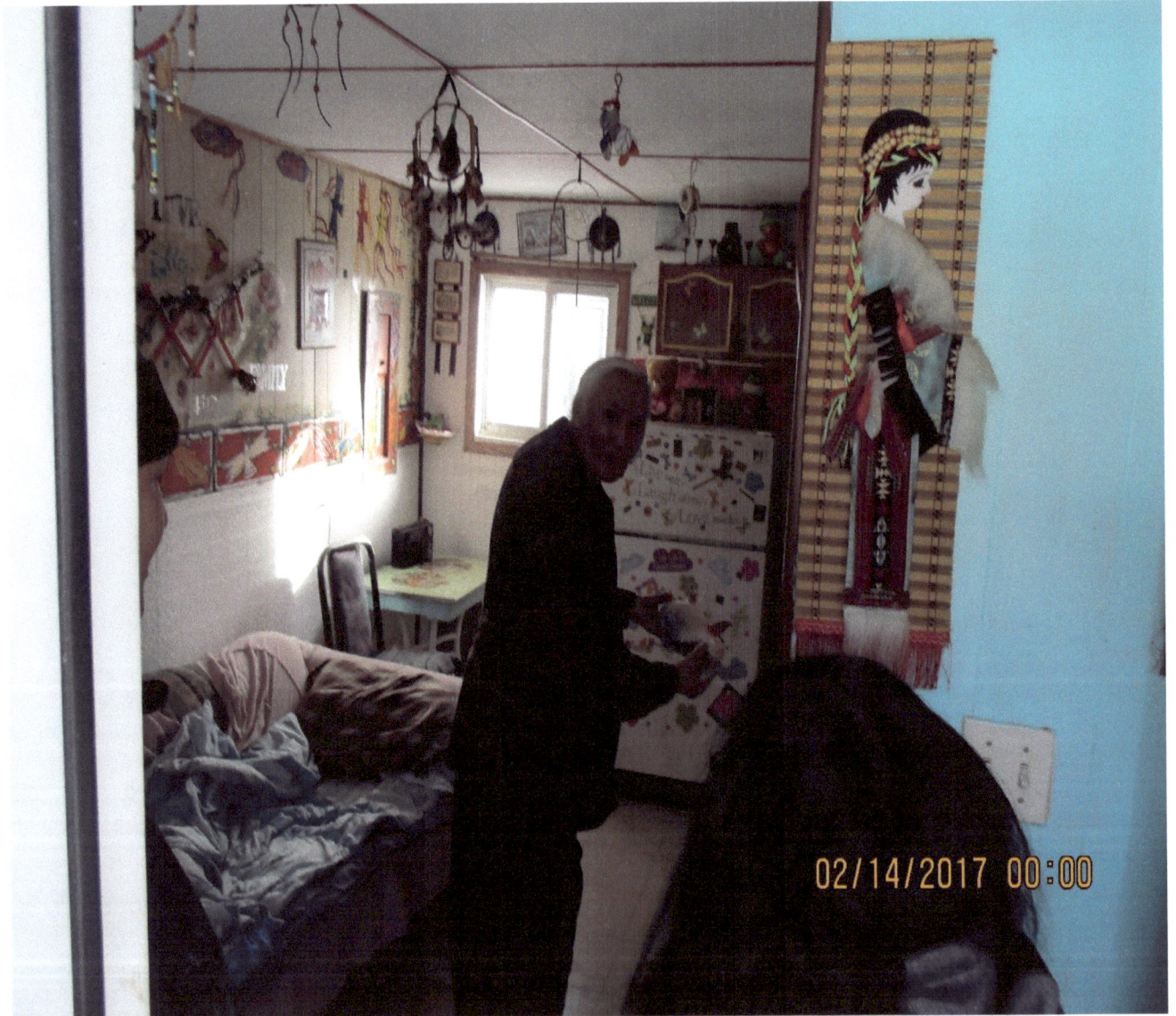

Bill (Wild Bill) Bighetty, w/ Sylvia.

Mr. and Mrs. Martin Colomb. w/Sylvia Caribou and Tyronne Caribou. (No relation)

02/14/2017 00:07

Bella Bighetty, w/ Tyrone Caribou.

Mrs. Margaret Linklater, w/ Sylvia, Toby, Pascall,

Ernie, Dhedra, Shelley, Tyrone and Roxanne.

Rose McCallum, w/Davey Francois.

About the Author

Pascall Bighetty

Born in Thompson, Manitoba raised in Pukatawagan and Duck Lake, Manitoba. Single father of two.Dedicated and proud member of the Mathias Colomb Cree Nation (Pukatawagan), treaty 6. Permanent resident, only left to attend other educational facilities.

I enjoy being outdoors from fishing to doing minor contracts, such as cutting logs. My knowledge and experience of the landscape has helped make outdoor activities a lot more easy and enjoyable. Raising my kids is one of my life joys and playing the guitar and simply help out when help is needed. Thank you and hope you enjoy my 1st book.